D1005925

Isaac Asimov
Master of Science Fiction

Karen Judson

Enslow Publishers, Inc.

40 Industrial Road	PO Box 38
Box 398	Aldershot
Berkeley Heights, NJ 07922	Hants GU12 6BP
USA	UK

http://www.enslow.com

Library of Congress Cataloging-in-Publication Data

Judson, Karen, 1941–
    Isaac Asimov : master of science fiction / Karen Judson.
        p. cm. — (People to know)
    Includes bibliographical references (p. 103) and index.
    Summary: Details the life and career of this prolific writer of both science fiction
and nonfiction who, at the time of his death, had written close to five hundred
books.
    ISBN 0-7660-1031-7
    1. Asimov, Isaac, 1920–1992. —Biography—Juvenile literature. 2. Authors,
American—20th century—Biography—Juvenile literature. 3. Scientists—United
States—Biography—Juvenile literature. 4. Science fiction—Authorship—Juvenile
literature. [1. Asimov, Isaac, 1920–1992. 2. Authors, American.] I. Title.
II. Series.
PS3551.S5Z73 1998
813'.54—dc21
[B]   97-36586
                                                                              CIP
                                                                               AC

Printed in the United States of America

10 9 8 7 6 5 4 3

Every effort has been made to locate all copyright holders of material used in this book.
If any errors or omissions have occurred, corrections will be made in future editions of
this book.

To Our Readers:
All Internet Addresses in this book were active and appropriate when we
went to press. Any comments or suggestions can be sent by e-mail to
Comments@enslow.com or to the address on the back cover.

Illustration Credits:
© Corel Corporation, p. 89; Courtesy of Janet Asimov, pp. 13, 61, 64, 67;
Design by Gary Koellhoffer, pictures © Corel Corporation, p. 86; July 1934
© Street & Smith, Greg Suriano collection, p. 30; May 1934 © Street &
Smith, Greg Suriano collection, p. 19; Photo by Jay Kay Klein, pp. 4, 7, 26,
33, 44, 54, 56, 70, 73, 77, 80, 82, 96.

Cover Illustration: Photo by Jay Kay Klein

Contents

Isaac Asimov

A Star Is Born

Imagine a world with six suns where darkness never falls. On this planet, because night never comes, no one has ever seen a star. Suppose that once every thousand years all six suns set at once. When that happens, the people living on the planet will know darkness and see stars twinkling in the night sky for the first time. Although the people have heard prophecies of darkness, they consider them the ravings of a cult and pay no attention. When the night actually falls, then, will they go mad, believing that daylight will never come? Will the people burn the cities, desperately trying to bring back the light? In the panic that follows, will their world be destroyed?

Isaac Asimov, renowned scientist and science fiction writer, used this plot for a story he wrote in 1941 when he was twenty-one years old. He credited John W. Campbell, Jr., editor of *Astounding Science Fiction* magazine, with giving him the idea for the story, which he titled "Nightfall." Campbell, in turn, had gotten the idea from the words of the poet Ralph Waldo Emerson (1803–1882): "If the stars should appear one night in a thousand years, how would men believe and adore; and preserve for many generations the remembrance of the city of God which had been shown!"[1] Asimov liked the idea and wrote the story, which Campbell then accepted for his magazine.

When the story was published in 1941, it set the standard for science fiction at that time. The story also established its author, Isaac Asimov, as a new science fiction writer to watch. In 1969, the Science Fiction Writers of America voted "Nightfall" the best science fiction story ever written.[2]

Over the next fifty years, Isaac Asimov, master of science fiction, also became known for his clearly written scientific and historical nonfiction. He organized and clarified new knowledge in astronomy, physics, chemistry, biology, and ecology. He explained Greek and Roman history, the Bible, Shakespeare's works, mathematics, and many other subjects both for children and for adult readers. In fact, during his lifetime Asimov wrote books in every one of the ten major Dewey decimal classifications used by libraries to organize books.

Asimov was famous not only for the clarity and

Asimov in his home office in New York City. Every one of the books in these bookcases was written by Isaac Asimov.

excellence of his writing but also for the sheer number of books he wrote. When he died of heart and kidney failure on April 6, 1992, at the age of seventy-two, he had written, by his own count, 477 books.[3] Since several books were ready for publication at the time of his death, and others, such as short story and essay collections, have since been published under his name, the count is closer to 500. Near the end of his life Asimov wrote of his production:

> *Over a space of 40 years, I sold*
> *an item every ten days on the average.*

> *Over the space of the second 20 years, I sold
>   an item every six days on the average.*
> *Over a space of 40 years, I published an average
>   of 1,000 words a day.*
> *Over the space of the second 20 years, I published
>   an average of 1,700 words a day.*[4]

To produce as many books as he did, Asimov did little else but write. From 1959 on, after he became a full-time professional writer, he wrote for at least seven hours every day of the week, including weekends and holidays.

Asimov wrote not to break records for the most books published, but to inform, to entertain, and simply because he loved his work. In June 1969, he wrote to a correspondent:

> *I write in order to teach and in order to make people feel good (for I am wedded to the theory that learning is the most enduring pleasure). It is nice to make money doing so. However, my chief reason for writing is to please myself, because I myself learn by writing. And that is my pleasure, too.*[5]

From an early age, Isaac Asimov knew that the two activities he loved most in life were learning and writing.

2

Child Prodigy

Isaac Asimov was born on January 2, 1920, in Petrovichi, Russia, two hundred fifty miles southwest of Moscow in the province of Smolensk. He was named after his mother's father, Isaac Berman. The name Asimov in Russian means "winter wheat grower," and family records show that Isaac's grandfather Aaron Asimov owned a mill. Aaron Asimov also owned horses and cows, making him a rich man by standards of the time.

Isaac's paternal grandparents, Aaron and Anna Asimov, had six children who survived infancy. Isaac's father, Judah, was born in 1896 and was the oldest of four sons and two daughters. He started Hebrew school at the age of five and not long after that was asked to do small jobs for the family business. Later, he worked at his father's mill as a bookkeeper.[1]

Isaac's mother, Anna Rachel, was born to Isaac and Tamara Berman in 1895. Anna's father died when she was six years old, and her mother remarried and had additional children. Her father had been married once before Tamara, so Anna had two sets of half siblings, as well as three full brothers. Anna's mother and stepfather owned a general store, and she began working in the business at an early age. She and her younger half sister eventually ran the store.

Isaac's mother and father grew up in Petrovichi. Judah was friends with Anna's three brothers, and the two knew each other all of their lives. As adults, they fell in love and were married in June 1918.

Isaac's younger sister, Marcia, was born in Petrovichi on June 17, 1922. Shortly after Marcia's birth, Anna Asimov's older half brother, Joseph Berman, invited the family to come to America to live. Since the Asimovs were of the Jewish faith, opportunities for them in Russia were limited. They heard that the United States was a land of promise. After a famine in 1923, the Russian government became more tolerant of emigration. Judah Asimov obtained permission for his family to leave what had by then become the Soviet Union.

In 1923, Judah, Anna, and young Isaac and Marcia settled near Joseph Berman's family in Brooklyn, New York. The Asimovs moved into a ground-floor apartment at 425 Van Siclen Avenue, in a neighborhood made up largely of Jews and Italians.

They had no electricity and no central heating. Gas jets supplied light in the apartment, and heat came from a cast-iron, wood-burning stove. Isaac remembered being happy there but said later that this was not a happy time for his parents: "In Petrovichi, my father had been a leading citizen, both socially and economically, and so had my mother. In Brooklyn, they were 'greenhorns.'"[2]

At first the Asimovs depended heavily on Joseph and Pauline Berman to help them learn American ways. As the years passed, however, they learned to speak and read English and became more familiar with their new homeland. The two families remained friendly, but gradually they drifted apart.

Isaac was the first in his family to learn to speak and read English. He learned that letters stand for certain sounds by studying street signs and asking older playmates what they meant. By the time he started kindergarten in February 1925, just after his fifth birthday, he could read and write.

Because five-year-old Isaac could read, his parents decided that he should not waste time with more kindergarten but should start the first grade in September 1925. When his mother took him to school on September 8, she knew he had to be six years old to enroll in first grade, so she listed his birthday as September 7, 1919. His age was never questioned until he was in the third grade and was asked to recite his birth date. When he said, "January 2, 1920," the teacher corrected him. He insisted he was right, and the school records were changed.[3]

In school Isaac learned so quickly that he skipped

grades. He had an excellent memory. He seldom forgot anything he read, so he always scored high on intelligence tests. (Asimov once said that he read all his assigned books the first week of school and was then educated for the year.)[4] Skipping grades meant that Isaac was usually the youngest student in his grade. Because he was so far ahead of his older classmates, he was labeled a "child prodigy."

Isaac got A's in school, but he made few friends. His friendships were limited after the age of nine because he worked in the family business and had little free time. He also had trouble making friends because he was more interested in the subjects taught in school than he was in his classmates. He was unpopular with many of his less gifted classmates because he often reminded them that he was brighter than they were.

Nor was Isaac a favorite of his teachers. "Early in my school career, I turned out to be an incorrigible disciplinary problem," he wrote in his 1979 autobiography. "I was not destructive or disobedient." He was simply so far ahead of his classmates in school that he was bored, and when he was bored he talked. "That was my great crime," he said. "I talked in school."[5]

For three years after the Asimov family arrived in the United States, Isaac's father, Judah, had worked at various jobs. To support his family, he was a knitter in a sweater factory, he sold sponges, and he demonstrated vacuum cleaners. In 1926, when Isaac was in the first grade, the Asimovs had moved to an upstairs apartment at 434 Miller Avenue in Brooklyn.

Asimov's parents, Judah and Anna, shown here, emigrated from Russia in 1923. Behind them is a photo of Isaac Asimov as a young man.

The new apartment was an improvement because it had electricity and a gas range.

Also in 1926, the Asimovs used their savings to buy a candy store in Brooklyn, at 751 Sutter Avenue, just around the corner from their apartment. For seven days a week, from 6:00 A.M. to 1:00 A.M., Isaac's parents sold candy, soda, newspapers, magazines, stamps, and cigarettes. (The store was closed only three days during the year, for two Jewish holidays: the first two days of Passover and on Yom Kippur.) From that time on, Asimov family life revolved around long hours spent working in the store.

In September 1928, less than six years after

emigrating from Russia, Judah Asimov became a naturalized United States citizen. Marcia and Isaac Asimov were listed in their father's passport and citizenship papers, allowing them to become American citizens at the same time as their father. (Because she feared answering the questions asked of those applying for citizenship, Anna Asimov put it off. She did not become a naturalized American citizen until 1938.)

A few months later, in December 1928, Judah Asimov sold the store on Sutter Avenue and purchased a larger store at 651 Essex Street in Brooklyn. The family moved into an upstairs apartment over the new store.

The Great Depression began in the United States in October 1929, and many people were out of work. Those who did have jobs had little money to spend. Like many families at that time, the Asimovs had a hard life. From the age of nine, Isaac worked in his parents' candy store every day after school, all day Saturday and Sunday, and through his three-month summer vacations from school.

Isaac's duties increased when his brother, Stanley, was born on July 25, 1929. After the birth of his baby brother, Isaac not only worked in the candy store but also tended his brother while his parents worked. Later in his life Asimov said that he learned to value work from his days in the store. "I am forever and always in the candy store, and the work must be done."[6]

Isaac's world was greatly enriched when he discovered the public library. Because his home was located on the boundary line of two of New York City's boroughs, Isaac qualified for membership in two public libraries—the Brooklyn Public Library and the Queens Public Library. The Queens Public Library was two miles from his home, but he walked the distance every week, in all kinds of weather. He was allowed to check out two books at a time—one fiction, one nonfiction—and he read constantly. Isaac even read while walking to and from the library, so that often he did not recognize acquaintances or customers from the candy store when he passed them on the street.

As an adult, Asimov wrote of his relationship with libraries: "During my childhood as a member of an ambitious but very poor immigrant family, I did all my reading and obtained nine-tenths of my learning in the public library. It frightens me to think what I might have become—and what I might have *failed* to become—without one."[7]

3

Higher Education

As Isaac grew, he had little free time to play with classmates after school, but he stole moments to read. When he was nine, he discovered the science fiction magazines his father purchased to sell at the newsstand. He could not take them home to read, because his father thought them trashy and would not allow it. Instead, Isaac read the magazines when he was alone in the store.

Isaac read every science fiction magazine that passed through the candy store. Two of his favorites were *Amazing Stories* and *Astounding Stories*. Reading the magazines in the store was a luxury, since Isaac could not have paid twenty cents each for them, as he would have had to do if his father had not owned the newsstand. Isaac tired of reading the science fiction magazines in secret, however, and he convinced his father that he should be allowed to read them for their scientific content. He promised not to crease or soil the pages, so the magazines could still be sold or returned to the publisher for a refund if they were not purchased by customers.

Isaac read constantly. He read books about Greek myths, European and American history, geography, mathematics, astronomy, physics, travel, and folklore. He read the fiction series popular in the 1920s—*The Bobbsey Twins, Pee Wee Wilson, The Darewell Chums,* and *The Rover Boys.* He read fiction by E. Nesbit, Charles Dickens, Louisa May Alcott, Mark Twain, Edgar Allan Poe, and Robert Louis Stevenson. He also read Mary Wollstonecraft Shelley's *Frankenstein* and the early science fiction of Edward Bellamy, Edgar Rice Burroughs, Jules Verne, and Herbert George (H. G.) Wells. He enjoyed mysteries and humor and read all the books and stories he could find by Agatha Christie and P. G. Wodehouse.

In fact, Isaac so loved the books he read that he yearned to own them, but he had no money to spend on books. He tried copying in a notebook, by hand, the books he especially liked. That plan failed when he realized it would take years to copy one book and his fingers would be forever cramped in the process.

The reading and writing Isaac did out of school helped him in school. He could read and spell any word, and he continued to progress quickly through the elementary grades. He entered East New York Junior High School on Sutter Avenue in 1930, at ten

As a young boy, Isaac Asimov loved to read science fiction magazines, especially Astounding Stories *and* Amazing Stories.

years of age. He was enrolled in the rapid-advance course for exceptional students, which meant that at the end of his first year in junior high he had completed both seventh and eighth grades. He started high school, ninth grade, in 1931 at age eleven.

The same year Isaac entered high school, he decided that the solution to the problem of owning books was to write new books that would be his to keep. He bought a nickel notebook and began to write, in pencil, a book that he planned as the first of a series. He called it "The Greenville Chums at College." Isaac abandoned the book after completing eight chapters, for he realized that he knew nothing about college students or going to college.

Isaac's first act as a high school freshman was to rush to the public library and request an adult card, which was available to high school students. The new card allowed him to browse the adult book section, but because the card was stamped "H.S." for "high school," he was still limited to checking out two books at a time. As before, at least one had to be nonfiction.

Isaac's father, meanwhile, was thinking ahead to his son's college education. He wanted Isaac to be a doctor. Judah Asimov knew that competition for medical school would be great. It would help Isaac's chances, his father reasoned, if he attended a prestigious high school. Boys High School of Brooklyn was such a school and Isaac began the tenth grade there in September 1932, when he was twelve years old.

His classmates at Boys High School were all older, and Isaac found that he was no longer the smartest student in school. In fact, at least a dozen students earned higher grades than he did.[1] Isaac's time after school was spent at work. His good grades were due more to his quick understanding and excellent memory than to time spent studying.

In early 1933, while Isaac was in the tenth grade at Boys High School, the Asimovs moved again. They purchased another candy store, at 1312 Decatur Street in the Ridgewood section of Brooklyn. As before, they lived in an apartment over the store. By this time, his father no longer objected to Isaac's reading the newsstand magazines, and Isaac read them all—from science fiction to the adventures of heroes like "The Shadow," "Doc Savage," and "The Spider."

For the first time since coming to New York, the Asimovs did not live in a Jewish neighborhood. Ridgewood was mostly Roman Catholic. The significance for Isaac was that, for the first time, he experienced anti-Semitism—prejudice against Jews. The Asimovs were sometimes called names and otherwise made to feel like outsiders.[2]

The Asimovs settled into their new apartment on Decatur Street. The family now owned a radio, and Isaac liked to listen to baseball games (he was a New York Giants fan) and to the popular comedians Eddie Cantor and Jack Benny. The new candy store was run much as before, except that Isaac now had to deliver customers' newspapers—both before and after school.

Isaac's life continued much the same, too. He went to school, worked in the candy store, and made regular trips to the library, with little spare time for anything else. Although he was not the top student at Boys High School, he was a very good student. Then in February 1934, when Isaac was fourteen and in the eleventh grade, the school offered a special class in creative writing. Isaac had always eagerly completed English class assignments to write term papers, essays, and stories and had received high marks for his writing. He confidently enrolled in the new class, but, much to his horror, he did not do well. In fact, the one time Isaac volunteered to read a composition before the class, the teacher humiliated him by using a four-letter word to describe his work.[3] "I never came closer in my life to giving up," he said later, recalling the incident.[4] Fortunately, he did not give up. When one of his essays was accepted for publication in the school's literary magazine, his determination to write was renewed.

Isaac graduated from Boys High School of Brooklyn in June 1935, at age fifteen. He knew he would have to go to college in New York City because he was still needed in the candy store evenings and weekends.

For Isaac, the logical choice of colleges was City College of New York because it was tuition-free and would accept any resident of New York City. But Isaac's father still wanted him to become a doctor and felt that a City College graduate would have a more difficult time getting into medical school. He wanted Isaac to go to a more prestigious college. Isaac applied for admission to Columbia College, a highly regarded division of Columbia University in New York City. He was granted an admission interview on April 10, 1935, and his father went with him. Compared with older high school graduates, Isaac lacked maturity, and he believed he made "a very poor impression."[5] In addition, although his high school academic record was excellent, he had not participated in extracurricular activities, so he was not as well rounded a student as many other applicants. Isaac was turned down for admission to Columbia College. He was, however, admitted to Seth Low Junior College in Brooklyn, a branch campus of Columbia University that was less renowned than Columbia College. He was also accepted at City College of New York.

Isaac decided, for financial reasons, to enroll in City College. Then, on his third day of classes there, Isaac received word from Seth Low Junior College that he had been awarded a $100 scholarship. The scholarship, plus a job with the National Youth Administration (NYA), which paid an additional $15 a month, would help pay expenses at Seth Low. Isaac quickly dropped out of City College of New York and enrolled at Seth Low.

Seth Low Junior College closed after Isaac's freshman year, but the school's students were told they could continue their studies at Columbia University's main campus at Morningside Heights in Manhattan.

As a college sophomore in 1936, Isaac continued to live at home. He found a job folding fabric onto bolts for $15 a week. He continued to work at the candy store when he was not in class or at his fabric-folding job, and he continued to read and write science fiction stories whenever he could find a few spare moments. His father bought him a typewriter in 1936 and he taught himself to type, so he no longer had to write out his stories by hand.

Because of Isaac's two jobs, school, and his writing, he now had less time than ever. In addition to his other duties, he walked a half mile every evening to pick up the late edition of the *Daily News*, which his father then sold in the candy store. Throughout his teenage years, Isaac's time was so occupied that he had no spare time (or money) for dating.

Isaac had enrolled in college as a premedical student, which at that time meant majoring in either biology or chemistry. One zoology course he took proved a miserable experience. He was forced to kill a cat for dissection, and the memory tortured him for the rest of his life.[6]

Besides hating dissection, Isaac found that he could make no sense out of objects under a microscope. He did not have a vision problem. He simply saw a confusing mishmash instead of the orderly structures his instructors told him he should see. Since biology would require hours of dissecting animals and studying microscope slides, Isaac decided to major in chemistry.

While Isaac was a sophomore in college, his father sold the candy store on Decatur Street and bought a new one (his fourth) at 174 Windsor Place, in Brooklyn's Park Slope section. A boy was hired to deliver the newspapers, with Isaac serving as backup in emergencies. The family lived in an apartment across the street from the store. The apartment was large enough that, for the first time in his life, Isaac had a room of his own, where he was allowed to keep some of the science fiction magazines he read. For years he had been returning the magazines to the newsstand after he read them, but now his father let him keep those he treasured most.

After his first attempt to write a novel, at age eleven, Asimov had tried again, several times. Each time he quit when the story lost momentum and he could think of nothing else to write. As he grew older, he concentrated on writing short science fiction stories, which were easier to finish.

Finally, on June 21, 1938, when Asimov was eighteen and a college student, he showed his first finished story, "Cosmic Corkscrew," to John Campbell, the editor of *Astounding Science Fiction*. He rode the subway to the magazine's New York editorial office and personally handed his story to Campbell. He presented "Cosmic Corkscrew" in person because his father had suggested that this was the proper way to submit a story.

"Cosmic Corkscrew" is about time travel. The subject had been done before, but Asimov's tale has an interesting twist. The story represents time as a helix, coiled like a watch spring. A time traveler can cut across from one turn in the helix directly to the next, moving into the future in exact intervals.

Campbell rejected "Cosmic Corkscrew" two days after he received it. He saw promise in Asimov, however, and continued to encourage and direct him. Four months later, after twelve of his stories had been rejected, Asimov made his first sale, not to Campbell but to Raymond A. Palmer, editor of *Amazing Stories*

Isaac Asimov tried to write his first novel when he was only eleven years old. Years later, when he was a well-established author, Asimov worked in his home office at the top of a thirty-three-story apartment building. He wrote in a tiny room, with all the blinds drawn.

magazine. "Marooned Off Vesta" appeared in the March 1939 issue of the magazine. The story is about three men on a wrecked spaceship and efforts to save them by devising a rocket to take them to the nearest asteroid. *Amazing Stories* also published the second story Asimov sold, "The Weapon Too Dreadful to Use." It appeared in the May 1939 issue.

At the age of eighteen, Asimov, a college student, sold his first story and was on his way to becoming a well-known science fiction writer.

Just as Asimov was in his youth when he began writing and selling science fiction stories, the science fiction magazines themselves were fairly young. *Amazing Stories*, founded by Hugo Gernsback in 1926, was the first magazine to specialize in science fiction. Gernsback referred to the tales in his magazine as "scientifiction," a label that did not catch on. He thought of the term *science fiction* after leaving *Amazing Stories* in 1929 to edit two competing magazines, *Science Wonder Stories* and *Air Wonder Stories*. (These two magazines soon merged into one, called *Wonder Stories*.)[7]

In 1938, when Asimov began submitting his stories for publication, there were many magazines called "pulps." The pulp magazines sold for ten cents each. They were nicknamed for the coarse, rough-edged paper they were printed on. There were separate pulp magazines for mysteries, Westerns, romances, adventure, horror, and other types of stories.

Stories written for the pulp magazines were known for their emotional or melodramatic style. That is, the authors who wrote for them typically created fictional characters who swaggered, swayed, staggered, danced with joy, and tore at their hair in despair. The fictional characters featured in the pulps did not simply say their words. They spat, screamed, swore, cackled, rasped, stuttered, shouted, and wailed them. Just three of the pulp magazines specialized in science fiction. They were *Astounding Stories, Amazing Stories,* and *Thrilling Wonder Stories.* (The name *Astounding Stories* was changed to *Astounding Science Fiction* when John W. Campbell took over as editor in 1938.)

Asimov's first contact with science fiction short stories was provided by the pulp magazines, and his early published stories were typical of the pulp style. The pay was low at the pulps—writers received just one-half to one cent for each word. Therefore, while writing for them, Asimov also learned to write quickly, to turn out as many stories as possible. He would go on to hone and refine his writing style, but for the rest of his writing career he seldom typed more than one draft of a story.

From Reader
to Writer

Throughout high school and college, Asimov was an avid science fiction fan, as well as a writer. Like most science fiction fans at that time, he liked to write letters to the magazine editors, commenting on the stories they published and the authors who wrote them. His first letter had been published in *Astounding Stories'* "Letters to the Editor" column in 1935. After that, his letters regularly appeared in the magazine.

Writing letters was fun, but science fiction fans also liked to get together in person for discussions. Asimov had heard of one such discussion group, the Science Fiction League of America, formed in 1934 by a group of fans, but he had never attended a meeting.

Young Isaac Asimov was always ready to express his opinions about science fiction and had many letters published in the "Letters to the Editor" column of Astounding Stories.

Then, in September 1938, a friend from Boys High School who belonged to the Greater New York Science Fiction Club invited Asimov to a meeting. Asimov was eager to meet some of the other fans who wrote letters to the magazines, so he made plans to go. (He still worked in the candy store, so he had to ask for the evening off and for money for transportation.)

Between the time that Asimov received his invitation to attend and the date of the meeting, members of the Queens group had a political disagreement. Some angry members started a new group called the Futurian Science Literary Society of New York, or simply the Futurians. Asimov's high school friend had joined the new group, so it was a Futurians meeting that Asimov attended on September 18, 1938. Asimov later wrote that in meeting other members of the group, he found "a spiritual home."[1] He became known as one of the charter members of the Futurians. Others included Frederik Pohl, Donald Allen Wollheim, Cyril Kornbluth, Walter Kubilius, and Robert W. Lowndes, all of whom became well-known science fiction writers.

Asimov first spoke before an audience at a Futurians meeting. His talk was the result of a radio broadcast by an actor named Orson Welles on October 30, 1938. The broadcast was based on *War of the Worlds*, H. G. Wells's science fiction novel about Martians invading England, but Orson Welles updated the story so it seemed to be an actual news report about Martians attacking New Jersey. Many listeners believed that Martians were invading, and the show caused an unexpected panic in the United States.

People were finally calmed when Welles returned to the air to say that the show was based on a science fiction novel and was not an account of true events.

After Orson Welles's broadcast, the Futurians held a debate: "Whether the Earth Should Voluntarily Give Up to a Superior Civilization or Whether They Should Put Up a Fight." Donald A. Wollheim spoke for the Martians. Isaac Asimov wowed the audience with a straight-faced humorous argument for the other side.[2]

In 1939, another important event in science fiction history occurred. Sam Moskowitz, a member of the Queens Science Fiction Club, planned the first World Science Fiction Convention in New York City. Asimov attended and in future years seldom missed the conventions when they were held in New York City. (Since that first gathering, the convention has been held every year, except during World War II, in cities throughout the United States. Today, science fiction fan clubs exist in several countries, and conventions are held frequently in various cities around the world.)

The year 1939 was also an important one in Asimov's writing career. Several of his stories published that year were firsts in science fiction. For instance, Asimov's story "Trends" appeared in the July 1939 issue of *Astounding Science Fiction*. The story is about the first space flight from the earth to the moon, which Asimov placed in the year 1973. (In 1959, the Soviet Union launched the first unmanned spaceship to reach the moon. Three American astronauts would actually land on the moon on July 20, 1969.)

Since 1939, science fiction conventions have become popular all around the world. Asimov was master of ceremonies at the Cleveland Tricon Science Fiction Convention in 1966. Asimov's friend Harlan Ellison won the Hugo Award for the best short story and expected Asimov to present him with the award. Instead, much to everyone's amusement, Asimov handed Ellison a bag of jelly beans.

Other writers had written about space flights to the moon, but in their stories people were always in favor of space flight. Asimov had observed, however, that people generally do not want to accept change, and he thought public reaction to the first moon flight would be negative. His story was the first to portray people as being against a flight to the moon. Asimov was nineteen when he wrote "Trends," and the technological details as he imagined them were later proved wrong. But in the fifties, when the first moon flight took place, Asimov found that his theory about public attitude toward space flight was proved right— many did in fact object to the idea.

Also in 1939, Asimov wrote a story called "Robbie," featuring a kindly robot. It was published as "Strange Playfellow" in the September 1940 issue of *Super Science Stories*. This story was a first, because other writers had always portrayed robots as monsters. The robot in the story was also different in that Asimov gave him a "positronic" brain. (Positrons are sub-atomic particles that have the same mass and energy as electrons but carry a positive charge rather than a negative charge.) Asimov saw positrons as a logical means for robots to think and react. He said he imagined that the positrons would move along "positronic pathways," briefly firing, much as nerve cells behave in the animal nervous system.[3] All of his robot stories after that feature robots who behave more like humans because of their positronic brains.

Other writers have followed Asimov's tradition. For example, the character of Data, on the television show

Star Trek: The Next Generation, is a "human" robot with a positronic brain.

Another of Asimov's robot stories was also a pacesetter. The April 1941 issue of *Astounding Science Fiction* contained his story "Reason," about a robot on a space station who refuses to believe that the earth exists or that robots were built by humans. John Campbell pointed out to Asimov the "Three Laws of Robotics" that he said he found in the story. From then on, all of Asimov's robot stories used these laws:

- A robot may not injure a human being or, through inaction, allow a human to be harmed.

- A robot must obey the orders given to it by a human being except when those orders conflict with rule number one.

- A robot must protect its own existence except when such protection conflicts with laws one and two.[4]

Other writers also used Asimov's Three Laws of Robotics in their stories. "I never minded that," Asimov said later in an autobiography. "On the contrary, I was flattered. Besides, no one could write a *stupid* robot story if he used the Three Laws. The story might be bad on other counts, but it wouldn't be stupid."[5]

In the context of his robot stories, Asimov had also introduced the word *robotics*. At the time, he didn't know he was inventing a word, he said. "I thought it was the word. If you will notice, physics ends in 'ics' and just about every branch of physics, such as hydraulics, celestial mechanics, and so on, ends in 'ics.' So I figured that the study of robots would be robotics, and anyone else would have thought of that, too, if they had stopped to think that there might be a study of robots."[6]

By the end of 1941, when he was just twenty-one years old, Asimov was no longer simply a science fiction reader and fan. He was now accepted as one of the field's most promising writers.

Asimov was recognized as a promising science fiction writer because his stories were unique. He created memorable characters as well as complicated technological plots. Moreover, in many of his stories, including "Trends" and his robot tales, Asimov seemed to foretell the future.

Readers of science fiction often marvel at the apparent ability of science fiction to see into the future. Men walking on the moon, the atomic bomb, supercomputers and robots, problems caused by overpopulation—all were topics for science fiction stories long before the events actually took place or the inventions were created. Of course, speed-of-light travel, galactic empires, and visits from beings from outer space are popular science fiction themes that have not yet come to pass. But who knows what the future will reveal?

Science fiction seems to predict the future when authors like Asimov have done their homework. Because excellent science fiction writers look closely at world trends in science and technology for plot ideas, their imagined worlds may parallel the real world. To ensure a constant supply of fresh story

Friendly toy robots like this one are part of Isaac Asimov's legacy. Asimov changed the image of robots in fiction. Other writers had always portrayed robots as monsters. Asimov created robots that were kind and acted more like humans.

ideas, such writers also keep up with technological advances and pay close attention to the world around them. For example, shortages of fossil fuels, long-term changes in weather, new diseases and the development of drugs to treat them, smarter and more efficient robots, advances in gene research—all stimulate writers to ask themselves, "What if?"

In short, when science fiction writers create their stories, they use events happening now to make intelligent guesses about things that could take place in the future. As a result, science fiction writers are sometimes able to imagine future changes that actually do come true.

Isaac Asimov frequently created situations in his stories that eventually came true, but he could not have foretold how quickly he would become a rising star in the science fiction field.

A Rising Star

By the time Asimov sold his first science fiction story, he knew he did not want to become a physician, but he also did not want to disappoint his father. Asimov graduated from Columbia University with a bachelor of science degree in chemistry in 1939, at the age of nineteen. He dutifully applied to five medical schools but was relieved when he was turned down by all of them.[1] (He applied to just one school outside New York City because he still worked in the candy store and could not leave home.) He was denied admission not because of his academic record, which was excellent, but probably because of his lack of both maturity and extracurricular activities.

Asimov believed he would not be able to find a job with just a bachelor's degree, so he decided to continue in school, to earn a doctor of philosophy degree (Ph.D.). But in what subject? He loved history but ruled it out as a graduate major, since he thought job choices as a historian would be limited to teaching on a college faculty, probably far from home, and probably for low wages. On the other hand, if he continued in science, he might be employed by a research facility and would probably be paid more.

With all this in mind, Asimov applied to do graduate work in chemistry at Columbia University. Throughout his years in school, some teachers and professors disliked Asimov, mostly for the barbed remarks he made in class and for his superior attitude. The head of the chemistry department at Columbia University was one of these.[2] Asimov was finally admitted to graduate school at Columbia, but not without some difficulty. He had to meet certain course and grade requirements the first year.

During his first year in graduate school, in one of his chemistry classes, Asimov met an attractive young woman named Irene. (In mentioning her later in his autobiographies, Asimov does not reveal her last name.) At twenty, he had his first date, with Irene. She soon finished her graduate degree and moved on, but Asimov would remember her fondly as his first love.[3]

By 1941, when Asimov was twenty-one, he had written thirteen stories. Only four, including the award-winning "Nightfall," appeared in print. Asimov recalled later that after February 1941, he never again wrote a piece of fiction that was not published.[4]

Asimov was a rising science fiction writer, yet he had never seriously considered writing for a living. In 1940, he had earned only $197 from the sale of his stories. He sold thirteen stories in 1941, bringing his writing income for that year to $1,060. Still, he was afraid he could never top that amount and he opted for security.[5] He decided that instead of becoming a full-time professional writer, he would continue in school and earn a graduate degree in chemistry.

Asimov had been a good student in high school, if not always the smartest in his class, and he was a good student in college. But by the time he entered graduate school, he recalled later, he was "simply no better than mediocre."[6] Other graduate students seemed better able to understand the textbook and lecture material and to apply the lessons in the laboratory.

The reason for the difference between himself and other graduate students in chemistry, Asimov decided, was that the other students had concentrated solely on chemistry. Asimov, on the other hand, had been interested in so many subjects that he had not studied just chemistry. He decided then, and remained sure throughout his life, that he was content to know something about "almost everything" rather than to specialize in just one area.[7]

Asimov would eventually earn a Ph.D. in chemistry, but his education was interrupted for a time. On December 7, 1941, shortly before he earned his master of science degree in chemistry from Columbia, the

Japanese bombed the United States naval base at Pearl Harbor in Hawaii. The United States then entered World War II, to fight against Germany, Italy, and Japan.

In February 1942, the twenty-two-year-old Asimov passed the examinations needed to receive his master's degree. He then received permission from Columbia University to continue for his Ph.D. Again, permission was obtained with some difficulty because, surprisingly, his final examination grades were not high enough to qualify him automatically.

Asimov did not volunteer for military service, but he was eligible for the draft. He was not drafted right away, however, because he would be continuing in school as a Ph.D. student. As a college student, Asimov had received a deferment that postponed his military service.

About the time that Asimov was accepted as a Ph.D. student, he was invited to attend a meeting of the Brooklyn Authors Club. He enjoyed the meeting and was soon attending regularly.[8] Joe Goldberger, a friend at the club, invited Asimov to double-date on Valentine's Day 1942. Asimov did not have a girlfriend, so Goldberger set up a blind date for him with a woman he knew named Gertrude Blugerman.

Asimov was struck by Gertrude's beauty. He thought she resembled the popular actress Olivia de Havilland. He had a crush on the actress after seeing her in the movie *Captain Blood.*[9] Asimov and Gertrude saw each other several times that February and he fell in love.

As Asimov was beginning his Ph.D. research,

more and more graduate students were losing their military deferments and being drafted. Asimov thought of looking for a war-related job. He did not want to be drafted, and such employment would continue his deferment. He had also begun to think of marriage, which meant he would need a steady income. Robert A. Heinlein, a fellow science fiction writer and Asimov's friend, was a former Navy officer employed by the Naval Air Experimental Station (NAES) in Philadelphia. He had been discharged from the Navy after becoming ill with tuberculosis. Heinlein had recruited L. Sprague de Camp, another friend who wrote science fiction, to work at NAES. When Heinlein offered Asimov a job at NAES as a chemist, Asimov accepted. He would be testing different products to be used on naval aircraft. The job paid a salary that would allow him to support a wife, and it also let him work for the war effort without going overseas to fight.

On May 13, 1942, Asimov took a train to NAES in Philadelphia to begin work. With this trip he left his father's house and the candy store for good, never to return except for visits. His brother, Stanley, then thirteen, took over Isaac's duties in the store.

Asimov put in six days a week at NAES. Every Saturday after work he took the train from Philadelphia to New York. He slept at his parents' apartment, then spent Sunday visiting Gertrude. On Sunday evening he took the train back to Philadelphia. Asimov kept up this routine for several weeks while he courted Gertrude. Then he proposed and she accepted. A few weeks later, Gertrude told Asimov that marriage was not a good idea. Asimov was

Asimov developed lifelong friendships with other science fiction writers. Here Asimov congratulates Robert A. Heinlein, left, for winning the 1975 Grandmaster Nebula Award from the Science Fiction Writers of America. In the center is science fiction writer L. Sprague de Camp with his wife, Catherine de Camp.

persistent, however, and the two continued to date. Gertrude finally decided to accept Asimov's proposal, and the couple set a wedding date for July 26, 1942. On that day, Asimov took his usual Saturday train from Philadelphia to New York. That evening he and Gertrude were married in the Blugerman apartment. Asimov was twenty-two; Gertrude was twenty-five.

The Asimovs spent a brief honeymoon at a resort in the Catskill Mountains near New York City. On August 9, Gertrude Asimov moved to Philadelphia into the rooming house where Isaac had been living. Four months later, the couple rented a small apartment.

Between working at his job with NAES and spending all his spare time with Gertrude, Asimov had little opportunity to write. His story "Foundation" had appeared in the May 1942 issue of *Astounding Science Fiction*, and the second story in the series, "Bridle and Saddle," was published the same month he began working at NAES. During his first year at NAES, Asimov did not write at all, then in 1943 he produced four more stories in the Foundation series for *Astounding Science Fiction*. The four stories were "The Big and the Little," "The Wedge," "The Dead Hand," and "The Mule." In the Foundation stories, Asimov satisfied his urge to write historical tales by making up future history, instead of taking the time to research actual history.

During 1942 and 1943, deferments from military service were not guaranteed for civilian workers at NAES. Asimov waited anxiously every six months to hear if his had been canceled or renewed. His deferment was eventually canceled, and Asimov was finally inducted into the army when the war was over, in November of 1945—just six months before he turned twenty-six, the cutoff age for the draft.

Asimov went through basic training at Camp Lee in Virginia. Then, because he could type ninety words a minute, he was assigned to clerical duty. In February 1946, the atomic bomb was to be tested on Bikini Island in the Pacific. Asimov was among a group of soldiers who were ordered to participate. Asimov's unit was first sent to Honolulu, Hawaii, to wait for orders to proceed to Bikini. While Asimov was in Hawaii, Gertrude's portion of his army pay was stopped after a clerical error indicated that her husband had been discharged. Asimov reported the error to his captain and was ordered back to Camp Lee in Virginia so he could straighten things out before his unit left Hawaii for Bikini. While at Camp Lee, Asimov applied for and received a discharge in order to return to his research. He was discharged from the army on July 26, 1946, with the rank of corporal, after serving a little more than eight months.

During his ten weeks in Hawaii, Asimov came to realize that showing off his intelligence made him unpopular. When he heard a fellow serviceman explaining, incorrectly, the workings of the atomic bomb, he was tempted to interrupt and set the fellow straight. He resisted the impulse, however, and found that he got along with his colleagues better because of it.[10] From this time on, he was less apt to broadcast his knowledge. As a result, most people meeting the adult Asimov for the first time considered him friendly and likable.

In September 1946, Asimov returned to Columbia University to finish his graduate work. On May 20, 1948, he passed his exams to earn his Ph.D. in chemistry.

Dr. Asimov accepted a postdoctoral position at Columbia, but the position was funded by a grant that ran out less than a year later. In January 1949, Asimov became a biochemistry instructor at the Boston University School of Medicine. He and Gertrude moved from Philadelphia to an apartment in Boston.

In 1951, Asimov was appointed an assistant professor of biochemistry. That same year, on August 20, Gertrude gave birth to a son, David. A daughter, Robyn, was born on February 19, 1955. A year later, the four-member Asimov family purchased their first house, in West Newton, Massachusetts, a suburb of Boston. The house had eight rooms, and Asimov used the attic as his office.

Asimov held the faculty position at Boston University until 1961. At the same time he continued to sell science fiction stories to various magazines. By 1958 his writing income was greater than his teaching salary and he no longer had to teach. Asimov kept his faculty title after 1958, however, simply because he was reluctant to give it up. After that date, he no longer received a salary from or taught classes at the university except for an occasional guest lecture.

In 1959, Asimov's first year as a full-time writer,

he published four books: *Nine Tomorrows*, *The Clock We Live On*, *Words of Science*, and *Realm of Numbers*. His income that year was $29,100—a large sum at that time.[11] Asimov was confident, now, that he could adequately support himself and his family on his writing income alone.

The Golden Years

While Asimov was finishing his education, serving in the military, and starting a family, science fiction was flourishing. In fact, the twelve years from 1938 to 1950 have been called the Golden Age of Science Fiction. Its popularity had grown because of the talents of such writers as Robert Heinlein, Cyril M. Kornbluth, Frederik Pohl, Donald Allen Wollheim, L. Sprague de Camp, and, of course, Isaac Asimov.

In Asimov's words: "That Golden Age began in 1938, when John Campbell became editor of *Astounding Stories* and remolded it, and the whole field, into something closer to his heart's desire. During the Golden Age, he and the magazine he edited so dominated science fiction that to read *Astounding* was to know the field entire."[1]

In 1938, the magazine, now called *Astounding Science Fiction*, featured a new type of science fiction. Before, the stories focused strictly on technology (gadgets) and predictions of scientific advances. Campbell had written stories under the pen name Don A. Stuart that added mood and character development to the science in the fiction. As editor of *Astounding Science Fiction*, he encouraged new writers to produce stories for the magazine that not only told of possible advances in science but also featured characters who reacted humanly to those advances.

The years from 1938 to 1950 were also a golden age for Isaac Asimov. Under Campbell's tutelage, he produced stories rich in characterization, and during this time he became one of the most popular and productive writers in history. In fact, Asimov emerged as one of the top four writers of science fiction. The other three were Robert A. Heinlein, Theodore Sturgeon, and A. E. van Vogt.[2] Campbell probably influenced Asimov's writing career more than any other individual in his life except his father.[3]

In his 1979 autobiography, Asimov explained that after 1950 he quit writing for *Astounding Science Fiction* because Campbell had changed. The editor had become interested in certain mystical beliefs he called dianetics and psionic powers, and he wanted the stories in his magazine to reflect those beliefs. Asimov did not like Campbell's new direction and looked for other editors who would accept his work. Asimov also split from Campbell because he did not want to become known as a writer who could sell stories to only one editor.[4]

Now Asimov's career branched out. There were more than thirty science fiction magazines, and many of them published Asimov's stories. In addition, for the first time in his career he began to write science fiction novels.

Until this time, most science fiction was published only in magazines. Around 1950 that situation changed. Science fiction had become so popular with readers that book publishers were eager to sign the best writers. The first phase of Asimov's writing career had been to publish stories in magazines. The logical second phase, then, was to write science fiction books.

In 1950, the Doubleday publishing company chose Asimov's first novel, *Pebble in the Sky*, as its first hardcover science fiction book. In the story, the main character, Joseph Schwartz, is blasted into the future by an atomic accident. Schwartz is helpless in his new environment, so a device is used to stimulate his brain. With his newfound intelligence, Schwartz is then able to form a plan to save himself and the galaxy from destruction. With this novel, Asimov's reputation as a top-ranking science fiction writer was secured.

By the end of 1951, Asimov had published two more novels. After 1951, he also expanded the series of stories called the Galactic Empire or Foundation stories that he had previously written for *Astounding Science Fiction* magazine. The connected stories became three novels called *The Foundation Trilogy*.

In *Foundation* (1951), the first book of the trilogy, Asimov introduced a new field of study called "psychohistory." Through psychohistory, future reactions of large numbers of people could be foretold using mathematical formulas. In the book, Hari Seldon, a scientist, uses psychohistory to predict the collapse of the Galactic Empire. Seldon hopes to reduce the dark ages between the collapse of the old civilization and the rise of the new by forming two "foundations" or scientific institutes in different locations in the galaxy. He hopes the foundations will preserve human culture, so peace and prosperity can be restored in the future.

The second book in the series, *Foundation and Empire*, was published in 1952, and *Second Foundation* came out in 1953. The three books cover four centuries, beginning in the year 12,069 of the Galactic Era. The books were widely read and became classics in science fiction.

By 1957, Asimov had written twenty-four science fiction books. They included six books for children, featuring a character named Lucky Starr. During the same time period, four collections of Asimov's science fiction and other short stories were also published. The award-winning *I, Robot*, published in 1950, was a collection of nine of Asimov's positronic robot stories. The other three short story collections included *The Martian Way and Other Stories* (1955), *Earth Is Room Enough* (1957), and *Nine Tomorrows* (1959).

During science fiction's golden age, Asimov discovered an additional source of income that he enjoyed almost as much as writing. Since 1950 he had spoken at science fiction gatherings and schools and had steadily improved at public speaking. He did not write his speeches in advance. He simply organized them in his mind, then ad-libbed, depending on his glib sense of humor and his excellent memory. He claimed that he could time a talk to the minute, without once looking at his watch. Then in 1956, one of his faculty colleagues asked him to speak at a PTA meeting. Asimov agreed and was amazed when he received $10 for his efforts.[5] From this time on, he was in demand as a paid speaker, though he seldom traveled outside New York. His speaker's fees increased with his fame.

At the same time, Asimov found that he could make more money with his nonfiction than with fiction. (Despite the huge number of stories he had written, he reported that as of December 1949, all his published works had earned him a total of $12,000.)[6] Asimov also realized that because of his remarkable memory, writing nonfiction was more enjoyable for him than writing fiction. He could simply sit down at his typewriter and write nonfiction, whereas science fiction required him to construct elaborate worlds and complex plots. As a result, he concentrated more and more on writing nonfiction.

Of the thirty-three books Asimov wrote between 1950 and 1960, twenty were fiction. The remaining thirteen were nonfiction: one on general science, one math, one astronomy, six chemistry and biochemistry, one physics, one biology, and one science essay collection. His first nonfiction book was a co-authored textbook for chemistry students, *Biochemistry and*

Asimov enjoyed public speaking almost as much as he did writing. Thanks to his sharp memory and glib sense of humor, Asimov's talks were in great demand over the years.

Human Metabolism, published in 1952. One of Asimov's most acclaimed books about science, written for the nonscientist, was *The Intelligent Man's Guide to Science,* published in 1960.

Asimov is noted for his ability to write about complicated scientific and technical subjects in words the average reader can understand. In his nonfiction for adults and for children, he made astronomy, physics, chemistry, biology, ecology, and mathematics come alive for readers who had little previous knowledge of those subjects. In fact, *Asimov's New Guide to Science* (1984) is ranked among the best science books written for nonscientists.

While Asimov's writing career was thriving, his family life was not. As their two children grew, Asimov and his wife, Gertrude, grew apart. He sensed as early as 1955 that Gertrude was not happy. He could not blame her; he knew his faults. All day long he did nothing but write. He didn't like to travel, was not handy around the house, and knew little about such things as mortgages and investments. His life was complete with his writing, and he thought perhaps he could never make Gertrude happy. Divorce crossed his mind, but he knew he did not want to leave his two children.[7]

The more unhappy his home life became, the more Asimov worked, which increased Gertrude's discontent. Both he and Gertrude raised the question of divorce from time to time, but both thought it best to stay together until the children were older.

While he was writing novels and nonfiction books, Asimov continued to write for magazines, but

Isaac Asimov with wife Gertrude, son David, and daughter Robyn at the Boskone Science Fiction Convention in Boston in 1965.

beginning in the late 1950s and continuing into the 1960s the markets for short fiction changed. The pulp magazines that published mostly fiction were gone. The new "slick" magazines (so named for the slick, shiny paper they were printed on) published little fiction. In *Asimov on Science Fiction* (1981), Asimov wrote: "Young writers, looking about, found almost no flourishing fiction market, except science fiction. As a result, the 1960s saw the rise of new writers who lacked knowledge of science and even sympathy for science, but who wrote science fiction because that was all there was."[8]

A "New Wave" of science fiction writers became popular. They experimented with new writing styles, where stories had no definite beginning, middle, and end. They also expressed new ideas concerning the future of the earth and its inhabitants. The old, generally positive views about the earth's future held by science fiction writers in the 1930s and 1940s were replaced by New Wave themes of destruction and despair. Now science fiction stories were as likely to contain sex and violence as other genres—a marked departure from the past.

Asimov noted the changes and could see no place in the New Wave for his style of science fiction.

New Directions

Asimov had dominated the science fiction field since 1941, but after 1958 he wrote little science fiction because he now felt he was too outdated to compete with the new writers. In *Gold: The Final Science Fiction Collection* (1995), Asimov explains his long absence from fiction:

> From 1958 to 1981, a period of nearly a quarter of a century, I wrote virtually no science fiction. There was one novel and a handful of short stories, but that's all. And meanwhile, along came the "New Wave." Writing styles changed drastically, and I felt increasingly that I was a back-number and should remain out of science fiction.[1]

During his absence from writing fiction, Asimov

was content to write nonfiction books about science. Asimov also loved history, and from the mid to late 1960s he satisfied his urge to write history by producing six popular books on the subject. These books, for teenagers, were *The Greeks* (1965), *The Roman Republic* (1966), *The Roman Empire* (1967), *The Egyptians* (1967), *The Near East: 10,000 Years of History* (1968), and *The Dark Ages* (1968).

Then, in 1967, a chance remark made by a friend changed Asimov's mind about writing science fiction again. "The field has moved beyond me," he told Evelyn del Rey, wife of his friend and fellow writer Lester del Rey. "Isaac, you're crazy," she replied. "When you write, you are the field."[2]

After Evelyn del Rey's remark, Asimov never again hesitated to compete with the new science fiction writers. His nonfiction science books still outnumbered his novels, but he no longer suffered from self-doubt when he wanted to write fiction. "If I had to, or if I felt like it, I wrote it," he claimed, "and if there were even the slightest danger of my feeling self-doubtful, I would mutter to myself, 'Isaac, when you write, you are the field.'"[3]

Although Asimov wrote little science fiction in the 1960s, his past work was so popular that in poll after poll, readers named him one of the top three authors in the field at that time. The other two were Robert A. Heinlein and Arthur C. Clarke.[4] (Of the big four of the 1930s and 1940s, only Asimov and Heinlein remained. Theodore Sturgeon and A. E. van Vogt had stopped writing.)

The top three science fiction authors were all

Some of the stars of the science fiction world at a gathering in the 1950s (from left): Lester del Rey, Evelyn del Rey, Harry Harrison, Isaac Asimov, Judy Merrill, Fred Pohl, Poul Anderson, L. Sprague de Camp, and P. Schuyler Miller.

friends. Heinlein and Asimov met while both were writing for Campbell. They worked together at the Philadelphia Naval Yard during World War II and had remained friends. Clarke was a British science fiction writer whom Asimov respected because he was well educated in science.

Asimov had become more and more successful as a writer, but both he and Gertrude continued to be unhappy in their marriage. By 1970, when David Asimov was eighteen and Robyn was fifteen, Isaac and Gertrude Asimov agreed to separate after twenty-eight years of marriage. Asimov wanted a divorce, but at first Gertrude agreed only to a formal separation. Because Massachusetts law said he could not get a divorce in that state without Gertrude's consent, Asimov moved to an apartment in New York City. In New York state, after he established residency, he could legally file for a no-fault divorce whether or not Gertrude agreed.

While Asimov and Gertrude were separated, he began dating Janet Jeppson, a psychiatrist and writer he had met in 1956 at a science fiction convention. Jeppson had asked Asimov for an autograph, but because he was suffering great pain from a kidney stone attack at the time, he was never able to recall his first introduction to her. Later he remembered well meeting her at a Mystery Writers of America dinner in 1959. The two had much in common. Both wrote mysteries and science fiction, were highly intelligent, and had similar tastes in music, theater, and humor. After their 1959 meeting, they saw each other at various science fiction conventions and became friends. Eventually Asimov and Jeppson fell in love.

Jeppson convinced Asimov to have a thorough medical exam. His father, Judah, had suffered from a heart condition called angina pectoris, and Janet wanted Asimov to be checked to see if he showed signs of the problem. The exam showed no heart problems but did reveal a small cancerous tumor on Asimov's thyroid. The tumor was removed in February 1972, with no lasting ill effects.

Asimov and Gertrude divorced on November 16,

1973. David and Robyn would live with their mother (for a while, David attended a private boarding school), but Asimov could see them often. He willingly continued to support Gertrude and the children.

On November 30, 1973, Asimov married Janet Jeppson and moved into her apartment in Manhattan.

Asimov had already taken another new direction in his writing. He had always loved mysteries.[5] Many of his science fiction stories were also mysteries, and his novel *The Caves of Steel*, published in 1954, had successfully combined mystery with science fiction. Its sequel, *The Naked Sun* (1957), was also popular with readers. The two books featured a human detective, Elijah Baley, paired with R. Daneel Olivaw, his robot counterpart.

While Asimov's science fiction mysteries were popular with readers, he yearned to write straight mystery stories that were not science fiction. In 1969, he had sold a short mystery to *Ellery Queen's Mystery Magazine* (*EQMM*), but other attempts were rejected. Then in 1971, Eleanor Sullivan, an editor with *EQMM*, contacted Asimov and requested a mystery story. He happily produced "The Acquisitive Chuckle," a story about members of the fictional Black Widower Club. (The Black Widower Club was based on a real club that Asimov had joined, the Trap Door Spiders.)

Ellery Queen's Mystery Magazine published twelve Black Widower stories and announced the series was finished. Asimov was not finished writing the stories, however, and eventually wrote more than sixty-five

Isaac Asimov and his daughter, Robyn.

Black Widower tales. From 1974 to 1990, the stories were published, twelve at a time, by Doubleday.

In 1976, another literary first occurred for Asimov. Joel Davis, publisher of *EQMM* and *Alfred Hitchcock's Mystery Magazine*, told Asimov he wanted to start a new magazine, called *Isaac Asimov's Science Fiction Magazine*. Asimov would not have to edit the magazine but would write an editorial for the magazine each month and answer letters from readers. Asimov agreed, and the first issue came out in the spring of 1977. (In 1992, the name of the magazine was changed to *Asimov's Science Fiction*.)

As Asimov's career progressed, some of his books sold millions of copies. He was often asked to edit anthologies (collections) of science fiction stories and to write introductions to books written by others, because his name on the cover of any book was sure to increase sales.

In May 1977, at the age of fifty-seven, Asimov suffered a mild heart attack. However, he did not cut back on his rigorous writing schedule after his illness. In fact, he worked on his latest autobiography while still confined to a hospital bed. He lost weight after the heart attack—going from 210 to 175 pounds—and, with wife Janet's help, began to take better care of himself.

Isaac and Janet Asimov were friends as well as spouses, and in the 1980s they became co-writers when they worked together on a book for youngsters titled *Norby, the Mixed-Up Robot*. Janet Asimov had published science fiction novels and stories under her maiden name, and she was an accomplished writer before they married. Asimov wrote that he "polished" the first Norby book a bit but that Janet did 90 percent of the work.[6] The Norby book was so popular with young readers that the publisher, Walker & Company, asked for more. The Asimovs eventually published a series of Norby books. As with the first two books, all of the Norby stories were largely written by Janet Asimov.

In the 1980s, many science fiction writers moved into writing screenplays for the movies. This would have seemed a logical career move for Asimov, but he was not interested in Hollywood filmmaking. One reason was that many science fiction writers who wrote for films moved to California and Asimov did not want to leave his home.[7] Asimov also believed that the Hollywood lifestyle was a trap. "It lured a person into a lifestyle of sunshine and tans," he once wrote, "of barbecues and swimming pools—a life you couldn't afford unless you kept on working in Hollywood."[8]

Although Asimov had little interest in writing screenplays for films, he served as science advisor for the *Star Trek* television series and for the 1979 movie, *Star Trek: The Motion Picture*. He also acted as advisor for two short-lived television science fiction series, *Salvage 1* and *Probe*.

In 1980, the Doubleday publishing company sold the movie rights to "Nightfall"—the story that had made Asimov famous. Asimov did not write the screenplay, however, or take part in any way when the movie was filmed. He did not see the movie, which, when it was released in 1988, was a critical and commercial disaster.

Isaac Asimov and Janet Jeppson, who married in 1973, worked together on a popular series of children's books about Norby, a mixed-up robot. Asimov credited his wife with doing 90 percent of the writing.

The editors at Doubleday asked Asimov to write a fourth Foundation book. He resisted at first, since it had been a long time since he had written about the Foundation. After rereading the earlier three books in the series, he became eager to continue the story. *Foundation's Edge* was published in September 1982. The book made *The New York Times* best-seller list, and Asimov won the Hugo Award for it in 1983. The Hugo Award, named for Hugo Gernsback, is presented annually by the World Science Fiction Convention.

In 1983, Asimov's heart problems returned and he had triple-bypass surgery to repair clogged coronary arteries. He recovered well from the surgery, but both of his parents had died in their seventies—his father in 1969 and his mother in 1973—and Asimov began to fear that he had too little time left to write. He was aging, but rather than slow down, he continued to produce more work than ever before.

Asimov published a fifth book in the Foundation series in 1986, called *Foundation and Earth.* It, too, made the *Times* best-seller list. (Two additional Foundation books were later published—*Prelude to Foundation* in 1988 and *Forward the Foundation* in 1993.)

Asimov's career moved through stages with the decades: In the 1930s and 1940s he wrote magazine stories. In the 1950s through the early 1990s, he wrote mysteries and science fiction stories and novels, nonfiction books and articles, and was a consultant to science fiction television shows. Asimov proved, again and again, that he could write successfully on any topic and for any age group.

Asimov on Writing and Other Matters

As his career branched out in many directions, Asimov was often honored for his writing. From the 1950s through 1980s, he received fourteen honorary doctorate degrees from universities. He usually refused to list his awards for interviewers, but these are just a few of the awards he received between 1955 and 1989:

- 1955: Guest of Honor at the World Science Fiction Convention.

- 1958: Edison Foundation National Mass Media award.

- 1960: Blakeslee Award for nonfiction.

- 1963: Special citation at the World Science Fiction Convention.

For Isaac Asimov, the awards and honors came pouring in.

- 1963: Special Hugo Award for "adding science to science fiction." (The award was given for Asimov's science essays in the *Magazine of Fantasy and Science Fiction*.)

- 1965: James T. Grady Award, given by the American Chemical Society.

- 1966: Asimov's Foundation Series won the Best All-Time Novel Series Hugo Award.

- 1967: Westinghouse Science Writing award from the American Association for the Advancement of Science.

- 1973: Hugo and Nebula awards for best novel, *The Gods Themselves*.

- 1977: Hugo and Nebula awards for best novelette of 1976, "The Bicentennial Man."

- 1981: Locus Award for nonfiction.

- 1983: Hugo Award for best novel, *Foundation's Edge*, and Locus Award for fiction.

- 1985: *The Washington Post* Children's Book Guide Award for nonfiction.

- 1992: Hugo Award for best novelette, *Gold*.[1]

The more Isaac Asimov was honored, the more famous he became. The more famous he became, the more people wanted to know about him. The truth was, he lived a quiet life, sitting at his typewriter (later at his word processor) every day, working in his home office. Although his life seemed uneventful, people were curious about him. They wanted to know how he got his ideas for stories, what were his likes and dislikes, and what did he think the future held for human beings?

It was well known among his friends that one of Asimov's pet peeves was the misspelling or mispronunciation of his name. In fact, he generally wrote to complain to anyone who misspelled his name. The most common misspelling was to replace the "s" in "Asimov" with a "z." Asimov once expressed his exasperation in a story titled "Spell My Name With an 'S'," which appeared in the March 1957 issue of *Astounding Science Fiction.* In the story, the history of the world is changed when a physicist named Zebatinsky changes his name to Sebatinsky.[2]

Similarly, Asimov's joy in receiving the Nebula Award for the story "The Bicentennial Man" was dampened when he saw that his name had been spelled "Issac Asmimov." The Science Fiction Writers of America offered to replace the award, but Asimov refused, saying it was a better conversation piece with the misspelling.[3]

Also well known among Asimov's friends, acquaintances, and fans was his fear of flying, which was due to his acrophobia (fear of heights). Ironically, the writer who lived in a Manhattan apartment thirty-three floors in the air and who took readers to distant planets in space ships did not like to leave the ground. "I never take airplanes and I don't like to be away from home for long," Asimov told an interviewer in 1988. "It simplifies life—it means that I turn down all invitations to travel long distances and I don't often travel short distances. I stay here with my typewriter, my books and my quiet life. And I like it."[4]

Not so well known to others was Asimov's claustrophilia (love of tight places). His writing office was usually located in a small, windowless room in his home, and it was here that he felt most secure. "My total absorption in writing creates a warm artificial enclosing world about me (one without windows) that shuts out the harsh outside world . . . ," he once said.[5]

One of Asimov's pet peeves was the misspelling of his name. On his Nebula Award for the short story "The Bicentennial Man," the Science Fiction Writers of America made a double blooper with "Issac Asmimov."

Asimov's sense of humor was also legendary among those who knew him or heard his speeches. "He loved to tell jokes and humorous stories," said Jay Kay Klein, a science fiction writer and Asimov's friend since the 1950s. "He boasted that he could remember every funny story he had ever heard. But we were at a party once and I said, 'Isaac, do you remember this joke?' I told the story and he started to jump in with the punch line, but failed to do so; he had forgotten the story."[6]

Those who knew Asimov also admired his honesty. "When given an advance [payment] to do a book, most authors will keep that advance even if they don't do the book," illustrated Janet Asimov. "Isaac didn't do that. If he couldn't do the book, he always sent the advance back."[7]

Asimov not only sent back unearned advances, but he also refunded royalties (wages earned from book sales) when he thought he had been overpaid. In addition, he was so confident that publishers would not cheat him that he seldom read his book contracts.

In the many letters Asimov received, a frequently asked question was "Which of your stories and books do you like best?"

Asimov said his favorite short stories were, in order of preference, "The Last Question," "The Bicentennial Man," and "The Ugly Little Boy." He liked "The Last Question" best because the idea for the story excited him and he was sure it had not been done before. "It managed to tell the story of a trillion years of human development and computer refinement in less than 5,000 words," he said in 1990. "It was made into a planetarium show that knocked the audience (and me) right out of our seats."[8] In the story, both human beings and computers evolve into forms of pure energy and consciousness.

Asimov wrote "The Bicentennial Man" in 1976, when the United States was celebrating its two-hundredth birthday as a nation. The story is about a robot who wanted to be a man and reached his goal on the two-hundredth anniversary of his construction.

"The Ugly Little Boy" was one of Asimov's favorite stories, he said, because it is more sentimental than his usual "cerebral" style. The tale concerns a nurse who takes care of a prehistoric boy brought into the future by a time machine. Asimov claimed that he cried when he wrote the story and every time he read it after it was published.[9]

Asimov said that people never asked what his least favorite story was, but if they did, he would say "The Portable Star." It was published in the Winter 1955 issue of *Thrilling Wonder* magazine, but Asimov said he was ashamed of it. "I wasn't aware of what I was doing when I wrote it, but on reading it after it was published it seemed to me that I was deliberately trying to put sex into it to try to keep up with a new trend."[10]

Asimov said he most enjoyed writing the following five books:

1. *In Memory Yet Green* and *In Joy Still Felt* (a two-volume autobiography)

2. *Asimov's Guide to Shakespeare*

3. *Asimov's Biographical Guide to Science and Technology*

4. *Murder at the ABA* (a mystery)

5. *The Gods Themselves* (also his favorite science fiction novel). This novel showed Asimov's ability to create interesting aliens. The story features trisexual nonhuman aliens living on a world that exists in a parallel dimension to earth.

Asimov was also frequently asked which of his fellow science fiction writers he most respected. He said that his favorites were Arthur C. Clarke, Clifford D. Simak (who was also his wife Janet's favorite),[11] and Frederik Pohl.[12]

Because of the astonishing number of books Asimov produced, people were interested in his work habits. How could he write all those books? The answer was simple, Asimov said. "All I do is write. I do practically nothing else, except eat, sleep, and talk to my wife."[13]

While he spent most of every day writing, Asimov did occasionally leave his apartment. At various times he belonged to several clubs and attended meetings regularly, including the Dutch Treat Club (a dining society), the Baker Street Irregulars (a club devoted to Sherlock Holmes), the Gilbert and Sullivan Society, the Trap Door Spiders, and Mensa (a group for people with high IQs).

In addition to his club activities, Asimov and his wife, Janet, traveled by train to Florida and California for lectures and took several cruises to the Caribbean, Africa, England, and France. Asimov could be persuaded to travel on cruise ships because he was usually booked to present lectures to the passengers.

The Gods Themselves, *published in 1972, won the the Nebula Award for best novel. It was also Asimov's personal favorite among his many science fiction books.*

Because the plots of his stories were often complicated, readers liked to know how Asimov created them. Unlike many writers, when Asimov plotted a story, he did not use an outline. First he decided where to set the story. For instance, would it take place on earth, or on a planet near Alpha Centauri, the closest star to earth other than the sun?

Asimov then imagined all the details of that setting. Was the landscape stark and barren of all life? Were its citizens humans or a new form of life? Did the creatures breathe oxygen or some other gas? What other beings existed in this world and did they get along? And he would invent a complete make-believe world where the story would take place.

Next Asimov thought of a problem for his characters to solve, and then the story was off and running. But how do you get your ideas? Asimov was often asked. "By thinking and thinking and thinking till I'm ready to jump out the window," he answered.[14]

Because he was a respected scientist as well as a popular writer, people also asked Asimov questions about the earth, the universe, and modern-day technology. Do you believe people have seen flying saucers? he was often asked.

Asimov's usual answer was that he believed people had seen natural objects in the sky that they believed to be flying saucers. He further explained that because of the distances involved and the problems associated with space travel over those distances, it was highly unlikely that space travelers had visited earth. And if they had, why would they come in secret?[15]

Asimov said that for people to travel great distances in outer space, certain complicated problems had to be solved. Even if we could travel at the speed of light (186,000 miles per second), he said, it would still take many years to reach the nearest star and millions of years to reach the nearest large galaxy. And at the speed of light, particles as small as hydrogen atoms could strike a spaceship with enough force to damage the ship and kill the crew.[16]

A question that many interviewers asked was, did Asimov think computers would someday replace human beings? "I think we can be certain that no matter how clever or artificially intelligent computers get, and no matter how much they help us advance, they will always be strictly computers and we will always be strictly humans," Asimov once said. "And we humans will get along fine. The time will come when we will think back on a world without computers and shiver over the loneliness of humanity in those days."[17]

Asimov the scientist was often asked what he considered the greatest threat to the survival of human beings on earth. His answer was that overpopulation was probably the greatest threat. According to Asimov, the world's population doubles about once every fifty years. This meant, he said, that by A.D. 2554, the head count will be 20,000 billion. When this figure is reached, he added, "the average population density over the entire surface of the earth, land, and sea would be equal to the average density, today, of Manhattan at noon."[18]

And if the earth finally cannot support its population, did Asimov believe we will someday travel to the moon or to other planets and start new colonies there?

"In the twenty-first century we'll have to find a new horizon," Asimov once told an audience. "We'll go back to the moon, only not this time to just get on it and come back. We're going to establish a colony there, and we're going to have a group of people on the moon who will then be able to make long space flights because they're used to being cooped up and enclosed in an engineering environment subject to low gravity. And they'll work out other worlds in the

Asimov's son, David, far left, watches his father sign autographs at the Noreascon #3, a world science fiction convention in Boston.

solar system."[19] These worlds could include colonies living on orbiting space stations.

Asimov's books, articles, and essays reflected his hope that the earth's citizens would see problems and solve them while there was still time. "The best way to prevent a catastrophe is to take action to prevent it long before it happens," he wrote.[20] He believed science fiction could serve as an early warning for catastrophes.

Asimov's Place in Science Fiction History

Writing fiction is difficult because the writer must imagine a story with interesting settings and characters that readers find believable. Writing science fiction is especially difficult, because writers must imagine and create future worlds, or worlds in outer space or parallel dimensions that are completely different from our familiar earth.

In science fiction, cities may have tunneled underground or may exist on a planet's surface under transparent domes. People may have moved away from earth to live on orbiting space stations. Automobiles may have been replaced by magnetic hovercraft. Robots may perform all work, freeing human beings for other activities.

Writer Jane Yolen, president of the Science Fiction Writers of America in 1987, presents Asimov with the Grandmaster Nebula Award to honor his writing achievements.

Not only do science fiction writers have the difficult task of inventing new worlds, they must also populate those worlds—often with creatures that may be nothing like human beings. The creatures of science fiction may have skeletons on the outsides of their bodies, flippers instead of arms or legs, several rows of eyes or one single eye, or the ability to breathe gases other than oxygen. Often these fictional beings live in worlds with extreme temperatures, or with other conditions that are unfriendly to life as we know it.

Clearly, Asimov had the imagination, writing skills, and scientific knowledge necessary to write science fiction. And the fertile imagination that served Asimov so well as a science fiction writer was, in turn, fostered by the books he read.

Throughout his lifetime, Asimov read books on many subjects. Those that he especially liked he read more than once. It was inevitable, then, that his writing would be influenced by writers who came before him.

Many earlier writers whose books Asimov read had written science fiction stories, but they were not labeled as such. For example, in 1818, Mary Wollstonecraft Shelley wrote *Frankenstein*, about a scientist named Victor Frankenstein who creates a man (Frankenstein's monster) from body parts of the dead. The monster comes to life when Dr. Frankenstein uses new scientific techniques on the body. Several years before Shelley wrote her story, scientists had discovered that an electric current causes twitching in dead muscle tissue. Perhaps this experiment provided the inspiration that eventually became *Frankenstein*.

Asimov read the works of many other writers who also wrote tales about the nature of the universe or about scientific advances or changes:

- Edgar Allan Poe, best known for his horror tales, wrote "The Conversation of Eiros and Charmion" in 1850. In the story, two humans die and become spirits. The two spirits meet to discuss the recent destruction of the earth by collision with a comet. The resulting explosion has removed the nitrogen from the air, and the globe is burning in a field of pure oxygen.

- In 1886, Robert Louis Stevenson horrified readers with his book *Dr. Jekyll and Mr. Hyde.* The novel told of a scientist (Dr. Jekyll) who invented a potion that suppressed his good side and brought out the monster inside—the evil Mr. Hyde.

- Edward Bellamy's *Looking Backward, 2000–1887*, published in 1888, dealt with time travel. In the novel, the hero travels forward in time from 1887 to Boston, Massachusetts, in the year 2000. Here he finds a utopia—a perfect society. In the ten years after the book was published, many other writers also wrote about fictional utopias.

- Jules Verne, a French author, wrote several widely read science fiction novels that some consider the beginning of modern science fiction. *Journey to the Center of the Earth*, published in 1864, features explorers traveling to the earth's core. *From Earth to the Moon*, published in 1865, is about space travel, a concept few writers had imagined before. In *Five Weeks in a Balloon* (1869), Verne wrote about a make-believe balloon voyage in a craft that did not yet exist. In *Twenty Thousand Leagues Under the Sea* (1870), a scientist explores the depths of the sea in a submarine far more advanced than any in existence at that time.

- H. G. Wells, the first major writer of science fiction in English, is considered by many to be the father of modern science fiction.[1] He wrote more than eighty books, including *The Time Machine* (1895), *The Island of Dr. Moreau* (1896), *The*

Invisible Man (1897), and *The War of the Worlds* (1898). As with Jules Verne's works, many of Wells's science fiction novels were made into motion pictures.

- In the early 1900s, Edgar Rice Burroughs, best known as the author of *Tarzan of the Apes*, also wrote several science fiction series, some set on Mars and Venus. *The Land That Time Forgot* (1924) has been called Burroughs's best work of science fiction. Burroughs and Asimov wrote for many of the same pulp magazines.

Asimov knew well the work of the writers who came before him, but his science fiction was original. Most remarkable, he created engaging plots in his science fiction that offered readers an escape from reality without breaking the fundamental scientific rules of the universe. Asimov's work was scientifically sound. Perhaps because of John Campbell's early influence at *Astounding Science Fiction*, Asimov also introduced to science fiction characters who were more important than plots or scientific gadgets. He said that his science fiction had two important functions:

- to warn about what the future will bring if we do not change our ways; and

- to give young readers information that will encourage curiosity and scientific creativity.[2]

The most important aspect of science fiction, Asimov believed, is the possible reaction of human beings to change. "After all," he once wrote, "science

Throughout his life Asimov loved to read, and he was familiar with the many writers who came before him.

(and everything else as well) is important to us only as it affects human beings."[3]

Asimov believed that well-written science fiction has educational value, even though the facts presented in the stories become outdated as scientific knowledge advances. For example, say that a group of students needs to learn about the planet Venus. The best way to introduce the subject may be through fiction, such as Asimov's book *Lucky Starr and the Oceans of Venus*. The descriptions of the planet Venus are now outdated, but if young readers enjoy the story, they may be moved to ask questions: Could Venus have a planetwide ocean? Are there other planets in our solar system that could have oceans much like those on earth?[4]

"And *that's* the educational value of science fiction," Asimov said. Not that it always presents up-to-the-minute scientific facts but that it "stimulates curiosity and the desire to know."[5]

Asimov also earned a place in the history of science fiction by sharing some of the worlds he had invented with other writers. A publisher once suggested that Asimov invent a universe and let other writers develop stories within that universe. Asimov liked the idea and invented "Isaac's Universe." Writers who agreed with the publisher to use this universe in their stories followed these rules:

- Life was present on millions of planets within the universe.

- Each planet had its own life forms that did not exist on any other planet.

- Only six intelligent species existed:

  1. Earthmen.

  2. Water animals similar to dolphins.

  3. Insectlike animals that breathed low oxygen air and neon gas, rather than nitrogen.

  4. A snakelike animal with fringed flippers.

  5. A small, winged animal that could breathe thick air.

  6. A strong, blocklike animal with no arms or legs that moved slowly and existed on a planet with heavier forces of gravity than on earth.[6]

Several writers, including Asimov's wife, Janet, developed science fiction stories and novels that took place in Isaac's Universe.

Just as Asimov himself was known for the unique settings for his stories, Asimov's robots were unlike any in science fiction up to that time. Although Asimov's robot stories helped interest others in the concept of robots and introduced the term *robotics* to the English language, he was not the first writer to use the term *robot*. The word gained popular use in 1921, with the production of a play by the Czech writer Karel Capek. The play was titled *R.U.R.*, which stood for "Rossum's Universal Robots." In the play, an Englishman named Rossum mass-produces a line of mechanical human beings to do the work of the world. The term *robot* comes from the Czech word for "workers," or "slaves." In Capek's play, the robots

In science fiction, writers imagine and create new worlds.

develop emotions, then come to resent being used as slaves and kill the humans responsible.[7]

The play made robots popular topics for science fiction stories that followed. The robots were usually shown as mechanical monsters that worked against and eventually destroyed the human beings who created them. Asimov grew tired of the same old robots-as-monsters theme and decided he would rather write about a kinder, gentler robot. Instead of destructive monsters, Asimov's robots were kindly machines that functioned according to certain rules and did not interact with human beings only to destroy them. According to science fiction historians, Asimov's robot stories, as collected in *I, Robot* (1950), introduced four ways that human beings and robots could interact:

- "Little Lost Robot" shows humans who relate to robots as machines. In the story, human characters are frustrated by robots (machines) that do exactly what they are told to do.

- In "Robbie," humans are masters over a robot "slave," a kindly governess and nursemaid.

- The human character in "Liar!" is Dr. Susan Calvin, who has a mystical relationship with a mind-reading robot named Herbie.

- "Escape!" treats the machine—in this case a robot spaceship—as godlike when it brings its human crew through a deathlike experience.[8]

As they created their unique plots and characters, Asimov and other excellent science fiction writers often seemed to accurately predict the course of history. For example, Asimov's novel *The Caves of Steel*, published in 1954, describes an event that actually foreshadows the future. In the novel a robot, R. Sammy, is murdered by a weapon called an alpha-sprayer. This device uses alpha particles to disrupt the positronic brain of the robot victim, thus "killing" him. Scientists who read the novel in the late 1970s wrote to Asimov. They pointed out similarities between the method used to murder the fictional robot in 1954 and problems at that time with semiconductors (the building blocks for memory in computers). According to the scientists, when alpha particles struck semiconductors (which did not exist in 1954), they caused "thinking" or logic malfunctions in computer memory. When he wrote *The Caves of Steel*, Asimov's scientific knowledge had allowed him to describe a logical event that could happen.[9]

"Perhaps the most important thing I did as a speculator was to foresee the various properties and abilities of computers, including those mobile computerized objects called robots," Asimov once said. "As a matter of fact, I sometimes astonish myself."[10] For example, in a passage in the 1951 novel *Foundation*, a main character uses a pocket computer, which Asimov called a "tabulator pad." Although computers at that time filled a room, Asimov's description of a pocket computer would prove accurate.

Years later, after the invention of pocket computers, someone asked Asimov why, since he had foretold the device, he didn't develop it himself and make a fortune. "Did you notice, perchance, that I only described the outside?" Asimov answered. "I'll be frank, to this day I don't know what is inside. I have evolved a theory; I think it's a very clever cockroach."[11]

Asimov was kidding, of course. He often joked about himself, but his knowledge of science and many other subjects was extensive.

Asimov's Legacy

When Isaac Asimov died of heart and kidney failure on April 6, 1992, the quality of his work had already secured his exalted place in science fiction history. He left a body of work that has endured because it is as enjoyable and informative to read now as when it was written. Asimov was known for his simple and clear, yet entertaining, writing style. His work—both fiction and nonfiction—presented stories or scientific concepts in everyday language that readers could easily understand and enjoy.

Asimov was, above all, a storyteller. "He set things down clearly and distinctly, so that you could tell exactly what he was thinking," said Asimov's friend the science fiction writer Jay Kay Klein.[1] Klein said

Asimov did not use "purple patches" (flowery prose) as some science fiction writers did, and his work was better for it.

Klein once wrote a letter of encouragement to Asimov after critics had written unkindly about one of Asimov's books. In his letter, Klein compared flowery writing to plain, clear writing, using the analogy of a mosaic stained-glass window compared with a clear pane of glass. "A mosaic window is something you admire," Klein explains, "and a writer of this type writes in words that are admirable in themselves, but it is difficult to see through the words, to tell what is going on in the story." By contrast, Asimov's writing was of the windowpane variety, Klein said. His words create so clear a picture that readers do not notice the "glass," and can easily look beyond it, to follow the underlying story.[2]

Asimov liked Klein's mosaic/clear glass analogy and used it frequently, most notably in his autobiography *I. Asimov: A Memoir* (1994) in the chapter titled "Style." "Writing poetically [like a many-colored mosaic window] is very hard," Asimov wrote, "but so is writing clearly. In fact, it may be clarity which is harder to get than beauty. . . ."[3]

It was Asimov's clarity that earned him the nickname "The Great Explainer." "Isaac Asimov is the greatest explainer of the age," confirmed the late Carl Sagan, the Cornell University astronomer.[4]

Asimov's writing skills improved over the years, but his grammatically correct, clear storytelling style remained the same. Those who have studied his work say that all of his fiction has three elements in common:

- Most of Asimov's stories, especially the earlier ones, begin with dramatic conversation between or among the main characters, rather than with straight narration. In fact, some critics claim that Asimov used the technique too much, as, for example, in "Marooned Off Vesta."

- His stories reflect his belief that religion often hinders scientific progress.

- In his stories Asimov foresees, usually accurately, the trends and cycles of history.

Asimov's style of writing changed very little after 1960, but he accepted the dawning of a new day in science fiction with his usual sense of humor. In a 1988 interview, he said:

> *Well, you know, I'm a has-been. The stuff I write now is exactly what I wrote in the 1940s and 1950s, and we have people writing eighties stuff now, and that's what . . . the people who vote, vote for. Fortunately, the readers are interested enough to buy the books, so that the fact that I don't get nominated [for a Hugo] . . . might fill my eyes with tears and makes it hard for me to make out my deposit slips . . . but I can do it!*[5]

After his death in 1992, the editors of *Asimov's Science Fiction* published tributes to Asimov from famous writers around the world. One friend and colleague, the British science fiction writer Arthur C. Clarke, wrote, "He stood for knowledge against superstition, tolerance against bigotry, kindness against cruelty—above all, peace against war."[6]

Asimov once said that his favorite quote about

Isaac Asimov was, above all, a storyteller. In one of his last public appearances, Asimov spoke at the Science Fiction Writers of America Nebula Awards ceremony in 1991.

himself was from a book review by Professor George Gaylord Simpson, a paleontologist at Harvard University. Dr. Simpson spoke for countless readers who enjoy Asimov's work when he said, "Isaac Asimov is one of our national wonders and natural resources."[7]

"He has died," Pat Duffy Hutcheon wrote of Isaac Asimov in 1993, "but so very much of what he was and believed and valued will live as long as there are people to read and think and wonder."[8]

"He loved to learn and to help other people learn," said Asimov's wife, Janet, in March 1997. "Everything he wrote, whether fiction or nonfiction, taught him something and he hoped it would teach other people something. He got such joy out of that."[9]

Asimov often said that writing was his favorite activity. In a letter dated November 1979, he wrote, "I am so ill-rounded that the ten things I love to do are: write, write, write, write, write, write, write, write, write and write. Oh, I do other things. I even like to do other things. But when asked for the ten things I love, that's it."[10]

Clearly, the fact that Isaac Asimov loved writing above all else has proved society's gain. In the hundreds of books and thousands of articles, stories, and essays that he wrote, Isaac Asimov wished no more—and no less—for each reader than that he or she would read, think, wonder, and enjoy.

Chronology

1920—Isaac Asimov is born January 2, first child of Judah and Anna Rachel Asimov.

1922—Marcia, Asimov's sister, is born June 17.

1923—Asimovs emigrate to the United States and settle in Brooklyn, New York.

1928—Judah, Isaac, and Marcia Asimov become naturalized American citizens.

1929—Stanley, Asimov's brother, is born July 25. Asimov discovers science fiction magazines.

1935—Admitted to Seth Low Junior College, part of Columbia University in New York; publishes a letter to the editor in *Amazing Stories*.

1936—Seth Low closes; Asimov transfers to Columbia University's main campus.

1939—*Amazing Stories* publishes Asimov's first story, "Marooned off Vesta"; "Trends" is published in *Astounding Science Fiction*; receives bachelor of science degree in chemistry from Columbia University; enters graduate school in chemistry there.

1940—"Robbie" published as "Strange Playfellow" in September issue of *Super Science Stories*; first of the positronic robot series.

1941— "Nightfall" is published in September's *Astounding Science Fiction*.

1942— Begins Foundation series; "Foundation" published in May issue of *Astounding Science Fiction*; works as chemist at the U.S. Naval Air Experimental Station in Philadelphia; marries Gertrude Blugerman; earns master's degree in chemistry from Columbia University.

1945— Inducted into the U.S. Army.

1946— Returns to Ph.D. studies at Columbia University.

1948— Earns Ph.D. in chemistry.

1949— Hired as instructor in biochemistry at Boston University School of Medicine.

1950— First novel, *Pebble in the Sky*, is published by Doubleday.

1951— Promoted to assistant professor; son, David, is born August 20.

1952— Doubleday publishes first Lucky Starr juvenile book; first nonfiction book, *Biochemistry and Human Metabolism*, is published.

1953— *Second Foundation* is published.

1954— Asimov's novel *The Caves of Steel* is published.

1955— Daughter, Robyn, is born February 19.

1956— Publishes story he believed was his best, "The Last Question"; begins paid speaking career on the lecture circuit.

1958— Leaves teaching to write full-time.

1960— *The Intelligent Man's Guide to Science* published; nominated for National Book Award.

1962— Wins Boston University's Publication Merit Award.

1963— Wins Special Hugo Award at World Science Fiction Convention for science articles written for *Magazine of Fantasy and Science Fiction*.

1965—Wins James T. Grady medal for science writing in chemistry, awarded by American Chemical Society.

1967—Wins Westinghouse-AAAS (American Association for the Advancement of Science) Prize for science writing.

1969—Father, Judah, dies.

1970—Separates from wife, Gertrude.

1973—Wins Nebula and Hugo awards for *The Gods Themselves*; mother, Anna, dies; divorces Gertrude; marries Dr. Janet Jeppson.

1976—First issue of *Isaac Asimov's Science Fiction Magazine* is published.

1977—Wins Nebula and Hugo awards for "The Bicentennial Man."

1982—*Foundation's Edge*, first novel in ten years, makes *The New York Times* best-seller list.

1983—Wins Hugo Award for *Foundation's Edge*.

1987—Wins Davis Readers Award for "Robot Dreams"; wins Science Fiction Writers of America Grand Master Award.

1990—With co-author Robert Silverberg writes a novel, *Nightfall*.

1992—Dies April 6 of heart and kidney failure.

Selected Books by Isaac Asimov

Science Fiction

I, Robot, 1950

Pebble in the Sky, 1950

Foundation, 1951

Foundation and Empire, 1952

David Starr: Space Ranger, 1952

Second Foundation, 1953

The Caves of Steel, 1954

Fantastic Voyage, 1966

Nightfall and Other Stories, 1969

The Gods Themselves, 1972

The Bicentennial Man and Other Stories, 1976

The Complete Robot, 1982

Foundation's Edge, 1982

Foundation and Earth, 1986

Prelude to Foundation, 1988

Forward the Foundation, 1993

Science Fiction for Young Readers

Lucky Starr and the Pirates of the Asteroids, 1953

Lucky Starr and the Oceans of Venus, 1954

Lucky Starr and the Big Sun of Mercury, 1956

Lucky Starr and the Moons of Jupiter, 1957

Lucky Starr and the Rings of Saturn, 1958

Nonfiction

The Intelligent Man's Guide to Science, 1960

The New Intelligent Man's Guide to Science, 1965

Asimov's Guide to Science, 1972

Science for Young Readers

How Did We Find Out About the Universe? 1982

How Did We Find Out About Sunshine? 1987

Did Comets Kill the Dinosaurs? 1987

Why Do We Have Different Seasons? 1991

What Is a Shooting Star? 1991

Why Do Stars Twinkle? 1991

Why Does the Moon Change Shape? 1991

What Is an Eclipse? 1991

Is Our Planet Warming Up? 1991

Why Is the Air Dirty? 1991

Why Are Whales Vanishing? 1991

Where Does Garbage Go? 1991

What Causes Acid Rain? 1991

Why Are Some Beaches Oily? 1992

Why Are Animals Endangered? 1992

Why Are the Rain Forests Vanishing? 1992

Why Does Litter Cause Problems? 1992

What's Happening to the Ozone Layer? 1993

Chapter Notes

Chapter 1. A Star Is Born

1. *The Works of Ralph Waldo Emerson in One Volume Including the Poems, Philosophic and Inspirational Essays, and Biographical Studies* (New York: Walter J. Black, Inc.), p. 528.

2. Joseph F. Patrouch, Jr., *The Science Fiction of Isaac Asimov* (New York: Doubleday & Company, Inc., 1974), p. 19.

3. Sidney C. Schaer, "Science Writer, 'Robotics' Creator Isaac Asimov Dies," *Newsday*, April 7, 1992, p. 3.

4. Isaac Asimov, *I. Asimov: A Memoir* (New York: Doubleday & Company, Inc., 1995), p. 552.

5. Stanley Asimov, ed., *Yours, Isaac Asimov: A Lifetime of Letters* (New York: Doubleday & Company, Inc., 1995), p. 8.

Chapter 2. Child Prodigy

1. Isaac Asimov, *I. Asimov: A Memoir* (New York: Bantam Books, 1995), p. 5.

2. Isaac Asimov, *In Memory Yet Green: The Autobiography of Isaac Asimov 1920–1954* (Garden City, N.Y.: Doubleday & Company, Inc., 1979), p. 44.

3. Ibid., pp. 51–52.

4. Ibid., p. 73.

5. Ibid.

6. Ibid., p. 88.

7. Stanley Asimov, ed., *Yours, Isaac Asimov: A Lifetime of Letters* (New York: Doubleday & Company, Inc., 1995), p. 198.

Chapter 3. Higher Education

1. Isaac Asimov, *In Memory Yet Green: The Autobiography of Isaac Asimov, 1920–1954* (Garden City, N.Y.: Doubleday & Company, Inc., 1979), p. 118.

2. Ibid., p. 121.

3. Ibid., p. 135.

4. Ibid.

5. Ibid., p. 140.

6. Isaac Asimov, *I. Asimov: A Memoir* (New York: Doubleday & Company, Inc., 1994), p. 90.

7. Ibid., p. 43.

Chapter 4. From Reader to Writer

1. Isaac Asimov, *I. Asimov: A Memoir* (New York: Bantam Books, 1995), p. 62.

2. Samuel Moskowitz, *Seekers of Tomorrow: Masters of Modern Science Fiction* (New York: The World Publishing Company, 1966), p. 252.

3. Isaac Asimov, *Counting the Eons* (Garden City, N.Y.: Doubleday & Company, Inc., 1983), p. 34.

4. Moskowitz, pp. 256–257.

5. Asimov, *In Memory Yet Green*, p. 286.

6. Isaac Asimov, "Our Future in the Cosmos—Computers." On the Internet at <http://info.rutgers.edu/Library/Reference/Etext/Impact.of.Science.On.Society.hd/3/>

Chapter 5. A Rising Star

1. Isaac Asimov, *I. Asimov: A Memoir* (New York: Bantam, 1995), p. 59.

2. Ibid., p. 91.

3. Isaac Asimov, *In Memory Yet Green: The Autobiography of Isaac Asimov, 1920–1954* (Garden City, N.Y.: Doubleday & Company, Inc., 1979), p. 258.

4. Sam Moskowitz, *Seekers of Tomorrow: Masters of Modern Science Fiction* (New York: The World Publishing Company, 1966), pp. 252–253.

5. Asimov, *In Memory Yet Green*, p. 324.

6. Asimov, *I. Asimov: A Memoir*, p. 92.

7. Ibid.

8. Asimov, *In Memory Yet Green*, p. 328.

9. Ibid., p. 331.

10. William F. Touponce, *Isaac Asimov* (Boston: Twayne Publishers, 1991), p. 10.

11. Isaac Asimov, *In Joy Still Felt: The Autobiography of Isaac Asimov, 1954–1978* (Garden City, N.Y.: Doubleday & Company, Inc., 1980), p. 185.

Chapter 6. The Golden Years

1. Robert Scholes and Eric S. Rabkin, *Science Fiction: History, Science, Vision* (New York: Oxford University Press, 1977), p. 69.

2. Ibid., p. 51.

3. William F. Touponce, *Isaac Asimov* (Boston: Twayne Publishers, 1991), p. 7.

4. Isaac Asimov, *In Memory Yet Green: The Autobiography of Isaac Asimov, 1920–1954* (Garden City, N.Y.: Doubleday & Company, Inc., 1979), p. 588.

5. Isaac Asimov, *In Joy Still Felt: The Autobiography of Isaac Asimov, 1954–1978* (Garden City, N.Y.: Doubleday & Company, Inc., 1980), p. 72.

6. Barry N. Malzberg, *The Engines of the Night: Science Fiction in the Eighties* (New York: Doubleday & Company, Inc., 1982), p. 17.

7. Asimov, *In Joy Still Felt*, p. 32

8. Isaac Asimov, *Asimov on Science Fiction* (New York: Doubleday & Company, Inc., 1981), p. 110.

Chapter 7. New Directions

1. Isaac Asimov, *Gold: The Final Science Fiction Collection* (New York: HarperPrism, 1995), p. 147.

2. Isaac Asimov, *In Joy Still Felt: The Autobiography of Isaac Asimov, 1954–1978* (Garden City, N.Y.: Doubleday & Company, Inc., 1980), p. 418.

3. Ibid.

4. Isaac Asimov, *Asimov on Science Fiction* (New York: Doubleday & Company, Inc., 1981), p. 229.

5. Isaac Asimov, *I. Asimov: A Memoir* (New York: Doubleday & Company, Inc., 1994), p. 371.

6. Ibid., p. 364.

7. Slawek Wojtowicz, "Dr. Isaac Asimov Talks With Slawek Wojtowicz," 1988. On the Internet at <http://home.interstat.net/~slawcio/asimov.html>

8. Asimov, *I. Asimov: A Memoir*, p. 366.

Chapter 8. Asimov on Writing and Other Matters

1. List of awards is from two sources:

    a. "Asimov, Isaac," *Who's Who in America: 46th Edition, 1990–91*, vol. 1 (Wilmette, Ill.: Macmillan, 1990), pp. 114–115.

    b. On the Internet at <http://www.alt.books.isaac-asimov>

2. Isaac Asimov, *In Joy Still Felt: The Autobiography of Isaac Asimov, 1954–1978* (Garden City, N.Y.: Doubleday & Company, Inc., 1980), p. 77.

3. Ibid., p. 769.

4. Slawek Wojtowicz, "Dr. Isaac Asimov Talks With Slawek Wojtowicz," 1988, p. 1. On the Internet at <http://home.interstat.net/~slawcio/asimov.html>

5. Isaac Asimov, *I. Asimov: A Memoir* (New York: Doubleday, 1994), p. 131.

6. Author's interview with Jay Kay Klein, February 25, 1997.

7. Author's interview with Dr. Janet Asimov, March 4, 1997.

8. Stanley Asimov, ed., *Yours, Isaac Asimov: A Lifetime of Letters* (Garden City, N.Y.: Doubleday & Company, Inc., 1995), p. 224.

9. Ibid.

10. Isaac Asimov, *In Joy Still Felt*, p. 19.

11. Isaac Asimov, *I. Asimov: A Memoir*, p. 142.

12. Stanley Asimov, p. 224.

13. Wojtowicz, p. 1.

14. Isaac Asimov, *Gold: The Final Science Fiction Collection* (New York: HarperPrism, 1995), p. 254.

15. Ibid., pp. 151–152.

16. Ibid., pp. 139–141.

17. Isaac Asimov, "Our Future in the Cosmos and Computers." On the Internet at <http://info.rutgers.edu/Library/Reference/Etext/Impact.of.Science.On.Society.hd/3/>

18. Isaac Asimov, "Is Anyone Listening?" speech sponsored by the Population-Environment Balance Conference, 1989. On the Internet at <http://www.clark.net/pub/edseiler/WWW/asimov>

19. Isaac Asimov, "The Future of Humanity," speech delivered at Newark College of Engineering, Newark, N.J., November 8, 1974. On the Internet at <http://www.clark.net/pub/edseiler/WWW/asimov_home_page.html>

20. Isaac Asimov, *Asimov on Science Fiction* (Garden City, N.Y.: Doubleday & Company, Inc., 1981), p. 86.

Chapter 9. Asimov's Place in Science Fiction History

1. "Science Fiction," Microsoft Encarta 96 Encyclopedia, 1993–1995 Microsoft Corporation, Funk & Wagnalls Corporation.

2. Pat Duffy Hutcheon, "The Legacy of Isaac Asimov," *The Humanist*, March/April, 1993, p. 3.

3. Damon Knight, ed., *Turning Points: Essays on the Art of Science Fiction* (New York: Harper & Row, 1977), p. 29.

4. Isaac Asimov, *Asimov on Science Fiction* (Garden City, N.Y.: Doubleday & Company, Inc., 1981), p. 54.

5. Ibid., p. 55.

6. Isaac Asimov, *Gold: The Final Science Fiction Collection* (New York: HarperPrism, 1995), pp. 148–150.

7. Ibid., p. 164.

8. Robert Scholes and Eric S. Rabkin, *Science Fiction: History, Science, Vision* (New York: Oxford University Press, 1977), p. 182.

9. Asimov, *Asimov on Science Fiction*, p. 82.

10. Isaac Asimov, "Our Future in the Cosmos— Computers." On the Internet at <http://info.rutgers.edu/ Library/Reference/Etext/Impact.of.Science.On.Society .hd/3/>

11. Ibid.

Chapter 10. Asimov's Legacy

1. Author's interview with Jay Kay Klein, February 25, 1997.

2. Ibid.

3. Isaac Asimov, *I. Asimov: A Memoir* (New York: Doubleday & Company, Inc., 1994), p. 221.

4. Sidney C. Schaer, "Science Writer, 'Robotics' Creator Isaac Asimov Dies," *Newsday*, April 7, 1992, p. 3.

5. William F. Touponce, *Isaac Asimov* (Boston: Twayne Publishers, 1991), p. 101.

6. Bette Chambers, "Isaac Asimov: A One-Man Renaissance," *The Humanist*, March/April, 1993, p. 8.

7. Stanley Asimov, ed., *Yours, Isaac Asimov: A Lifetime of Letters* (New York: Doubleday & Company, Inc., 1995), p. 227.

8. Pat Duffy Hutcheon, "The Legacy of Isaac Asimov," *The Humanist*, March/April, 1993, p. 3.

9. Author's interview with Dr. Janet Asimov, March 4, 1997.

10. Stanley Asimov, p. 8.

Further Reading

Asimov, Isaac. *In Memory Yet Green: The Autobiography of Isaac Asimov, 1920–1954.* Garden City, N.Y.: Doubleday & Company, Inc., 1979.

————. *In Joy Still Felt: The Autobiography of Isaac Asimov, 1954–1978.* Garden City, N.Y.: Doubleday & Company, Inc., 1980.

————. *I. Asimov: A Memoir.* New York: Doubleday & Company, Inc., 1994.

————. *Yours, Isaac Asimov: A Lifetime of Letters,* Stanley Asimov, ed. New York: Doubleday & Company, Inc., 1995.

Erlanger, Ellen. *Isaac Asimov: Scientist and Storyteller* (Minneapolis: Lerner Publications Co., 1986).

On the Internet

The official Isaac Asimov home page:
<http://www.clark.net/pub/edseiler/WWW/asimov_home_page.html>

Another Asimov home page:
<http://www.stanford.edu/~afernand/>

Another Guide to Isaac Asimov:
<http://www.blueneptune.com/~tseng/Asimov/Asimov.html>

Biographical Information and Two Speeches made by Isaac Asimov at Rutgers University:
<http://info.rutgers.edu/Library/Reference/Etext/Impact.of.Science.On.Society.hd/3/>

Index